HERMAN SUNDAYS

The First Seventy-Seven Weekend Herman Comics in Full Color

by Jim Unger

Andrews and McMeel, Inc.
A Universal Press Syndicate Company
Kansas City • New York

ISBN: 0-8362-1176-6
Library of Congress Catalog Card Number: 81-70018

September 27, 1981

September 20, 1981

September 13, 1981

September 6, 1981

August 23, 1981

August 16, 1981

August 9, 1981

August 2, 1981

July 26, 1981

July 19, 1981

July 12, 1981

July 5, 1981

June 28, 1981

June 21, 1981

June 14, 1981

June 7, 1981

May 31, 1981

May 24, 1981

HERMAN
by JIM UNGER

HOLD ON.... I'D BETTER ASK 'YOU-KNOW -WHO'...

MY SISTER WANTS TO COME FOR THE WEEKEND.

FORGET IT!

ABSOLUTELY OUT OF THE QUESTION.

NOT IN A MILLION YEARS!

NEVER!

GREAT! WE'LL SEE YOU ALL ON FRIDAY.

May 17, 1981

HERMAN

by JIM UNGER

ANIMALS ARE ANIMALS!

THEY'RE JUST DUMB OLD GORILLAS....THEY DON'T UNDERSTAND ANYTHING!

YOU'LL MAKE THEM MAD!!

SO THEY GET MAD! ...WHAT ARE THEY GONNA DO?

THEY'RE FORTY FEET ACROSS A MOAT.

May 10, 1981

May 3, 1981

April 26, 1981

April 19, 1981

HERMAN

by JIM UNGER

MAY I HAVE A QUIET WORD WITH YOU?

BELIEVE ME, I HATE TO BE THE ONE WHO HAS TO DO THIS!

...BUT I HAVE SOME VERY DISTRESSING NEWS FOR YOU.

HOLD ON, HOLD ON! LET ME LIE BACK.

OKAY DOC., I CAN TAKE IT!

YOUR LATEST CHECK BOUNCED!

April 12, 1981

HERMAN
by JIM UNGER

DID WE GET ANY MAIL?

A POSTCARD FROM YOUR GRANDFATHER, SPOTTED-ELK.

HE SAYS HE HAS CROSSED THE GREAT RIVER AND HAS SEEN THE VALLEY OF A THOUSAND PINES.

HE WILL RETURN AT THE TIME OF THE SWALLOWS, IN THREE MOONS!

WHAT'S THE PICTURE ON THE BACK?

BO DEREK.

April 5, 1981

March 29, 1981

March 22, 1981

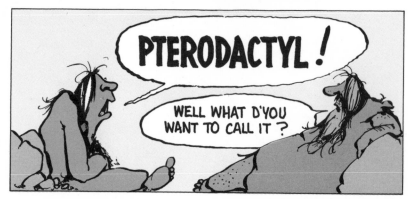

March 8, 1981

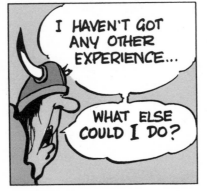

March 1, 1981

February 22, 1981

February 15, 1981

February 8, 1981

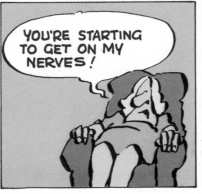

February 1, 1981

January 25, 1981

HERMAN

by JIM UNGER

I KNEW YOU'D FORGET TODAY!

SOMETIMES, I THINK YOU JUST DON'T CARE....

D'YOU KNOW WHAT TODAY IS?

OH NO! IT'S YOUR BIRTHDAY!

HAPPY BIRTHDAY DARLING. I BOUGHT YOU A BEAUTIFUL GIFT.... BUT.... I.... LEFT IT AT WORK.

I'VE BEEN PLANNING THIS ALL YEAR...

I'LL GO BACK TO THE OFFICE AND GET THE GIFT....

AND I'LL PICK UP THE CAKE I ORDERED YESTERDAY

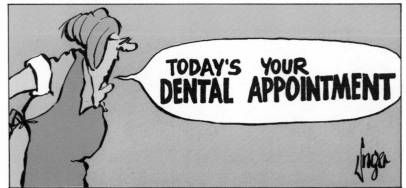

TODAY'S YOUR DENTAL APPOINTMENT

January 18, 1981

January 11, 1981

January 4, 1981

December 28, 1980

December 21, 1980

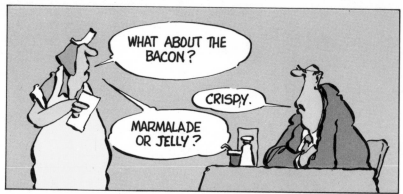

December 14, 1980

December 7, 1980

November 30, 1980

HERMAN
by Jim Unger

HI GRANPA.

GRANNIE SAID YOU USED TO BE A FIGHTER: HOW MANY FIGHTS DID YOU HAVE?

OVER A HUNDRED... I WAS ONLY KNOCKED OUT TWICE!

HOW MANY DID YOU WIN?

FIVE.

FIVE!... HOW COME ONLY FIVE?

SHE'S A LOT FASTER THAN SHE LOOKS!

November 23, 1980

DENTIST

HERMAN by Jim Unger

IS THIS YOUR FIRST TIME HERE?

GOOD GRIEF!

AAAAGH.

YOU DON'T TAKE VERY GOOD CARE OF YOUR TEETH.

AGH!

YOU NEED ABOUT TWO HOURS WORK!

CAN I LEAVE THEM HERE OVER THE WEEKEND?

November 16, 1980

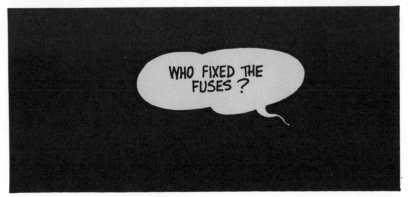

November 9, 1980

November 2, 1980

WALLPAPER SALE

HERMAN

by JIM UNGER

WE WANT SOMETHING TASTEFUL FOR OUR LIVING ROOM.

HAVE YOU GOT ANY WALLPAPER ...WITH RABBITS?

...PLAYING BANJOS AND TRUMPETS?

NOTHING AT ALL LIKE THAT!

WHAT ABOUT ELEPHANTS ON A PURPLE BACKGROUND?

...PULLING UP TREES?

DO YOU LIKE FLOWERS?

YOU CAN IMAGINE WHAT **HIS** HOUSE LOOKS LIKE!

October 26, 1980

October 19, 1980

October 12, 1980

October 5, 1980

September 28, 1980

September 21, 1980

September 14, 1980

September 7, 1980

DING DONG

WE ALWAYS GET VISITORS WHEN WE'RE EATING!

THERE'S A GUY AT THE DOOR SELLING COOKWARE.

TELL HIM WE DON'T NEED ANY.

I DID, BUT HE WON'T GO AWAY.

JUST SAY, "NO THANKS" AND CLOSE THE DOOR.

STAND ASIDE, I'LL SOON FIX HIM.

YOUR LUNCH IS GETTING COLD.

HOW MUCH WERE THEY?

August 31, 1980

August 24, 1980

August 10, 1980

August 3, 1980

July 27, 1980

July 20, 1980

July 13, 1980

June 29, 1980

June 22, 1980

June 15, 1980

June 8, 1980

June 1, 1980

May 25, 1980

HERMAN

by JIM Unger

May 18, 1980

HERMAN by JIM Unger

May 11, 1980

May 4, 1980

April 27, 1980

April 20, 1980

April 13, 1980

HERMAN

by JIM Unger

DINNER

YOUR DINNER'S READY

ARE YOU DEAF?

DID YOU HEAR ME? .... YOUR DINNER'S GETTING COLD.

HOW MANY TIMES DO I HAVE TO SHOUT?

DINNER

DO YOU ENJOY IGNORING ME?

April 6, 1980

March 30, 1980